MW00595338

David Carr Glover
METHOD for PIANO

THEORY

Martha Mier and
June Montgomery
with David Carr Glover

The knowledge of note reading, recognition of intervals, rhythm, music symbols and terms, and the ability to listen are essential to the development of a strong foundation for the piano student.

This THEORY book was written to help provide this foundation by giving students reinforcement of the concepts presented in the LESSONS book of the David Carr Glover METHOD for PIANO. As the students advance in their ability to play the piano, the THEORY book will help give them a better understanding of the music they are performing.

The pages are designed to be interesting and fun for the students in order to spark their enthusiasm and increase their motivation.

Teachers, please notice that the answers and musical examples for use with the listening exercises are found in the back of this book.

THEORY, Level One, is directly correlated with LESSONS, Level One, of the David Carr Glover METHOD for PIANO.

Design and Illustrations: Jeannette Aquino
Editor: Carole Flatau

Contents

Supplementary materials correlated with
LESSONS, Level One, from the
David Carr Glover METHOD for PIANO

THEORY .... Introduce with Page 4

SIGHT READING AND EAR TRAINING .... Page 8

TECHNIC .... Page 10

PERFORMANCE .... Page 11

Additional teaching aids include
Music Assignment Book, Music Flash Cards,
Manuscript Writing Book

Review

1. On the staff below, draw
    A.   a BRACE and BAR LINE at the beginning
         of the staff.
    B.   TREBLE and BASS CLEF signs.
    C.   a DOUBLE BAR at the end of the staff.
    D.   the notes in the C MAJOR POSITION in
         both clefs. Use whole notes.

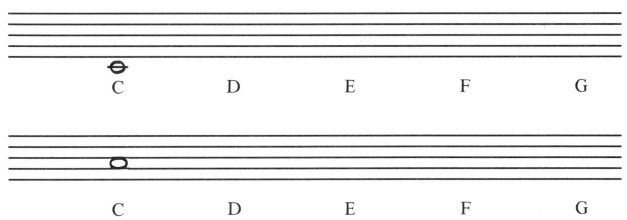

C   D   E   F   G

C   D   E   F   G

2. Explain this time signature.

    3 ◄——— means there are _____ beats in each measure.
    4 ◄——— means the _____ note receives one beat.

3. Write the number of beats each note or rest receives in $\frac{4}{4}$ time.

4. INTERVAL REVIEW: Write the name of each interval on the blank beside it.
                    (Write 2nd, 3rd, 4th, or 5th.)

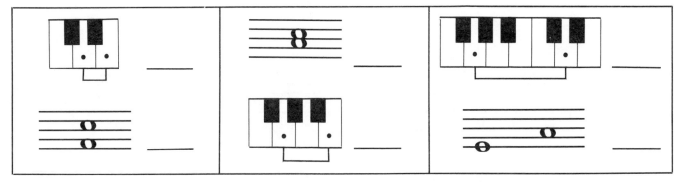

Use with pages 4-5, LESSONS, Level One.

Note Review

KEYBOARD AND NOTE CHART

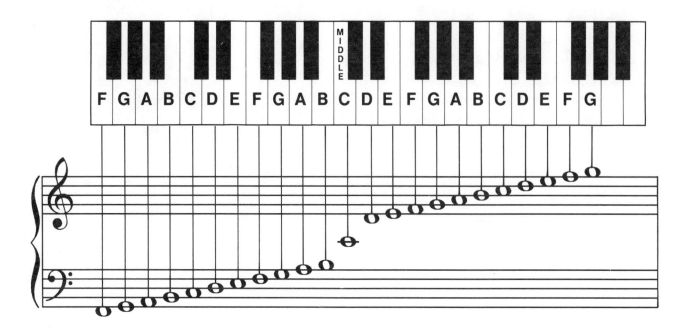

5. Write the names of these notes. Locate and play.

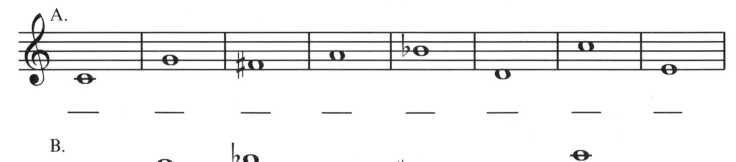

6. Write the names of these notes. They spell words. Locate and play.

Use with pages 6-7, LESSONS, Level One.

Half Steps and Whole Steps

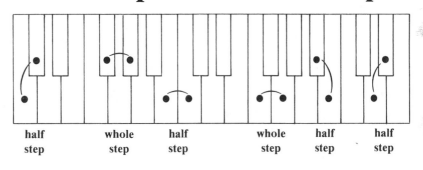

half step   whole step   half step   whole step   half step   half step

A HALF STEP is the distance from one key to the VERY NEXT key.

A WHOLE STEP is the distance from one key to another, with one key in between. (Two half steps make a whole step.)

7. A. On the blanks below this keyboard, write H for half step or W for whole step for the keys that are marked.

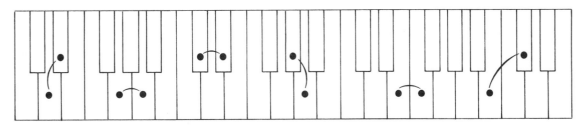

____ ____ ____ ____ ____ ____

B. Write H for half step or W for whole step for each pair of notes on the staff below.

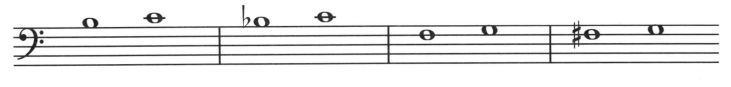

____ ____ ____ ____

The notes in the C Major 5-finger position form this pattern of half and whole steps:

WHOLE - WHOLE - HALF - WHOLE

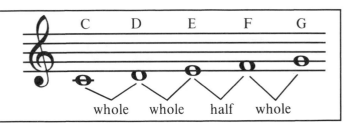

8. Name the notes below. Write W for whole step or H for half step under each pair of notes.

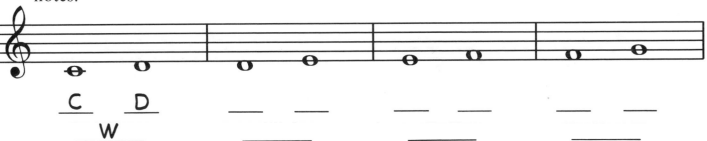

C D ____ ____ ____ ____ ____ ____ ____ ____

W ____ ____ ____ ____

Use with page 8, LESSONS, Level One.

C Major Position
(Review)

9. Name these notes.

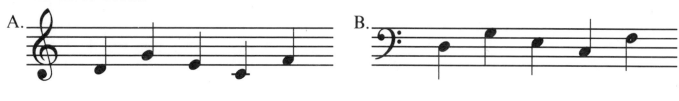

A. ___ ___ ___ ___

B. ___ ___ ___ ___ ___

10. Solve this puzzle by naming the notes in the "clues."

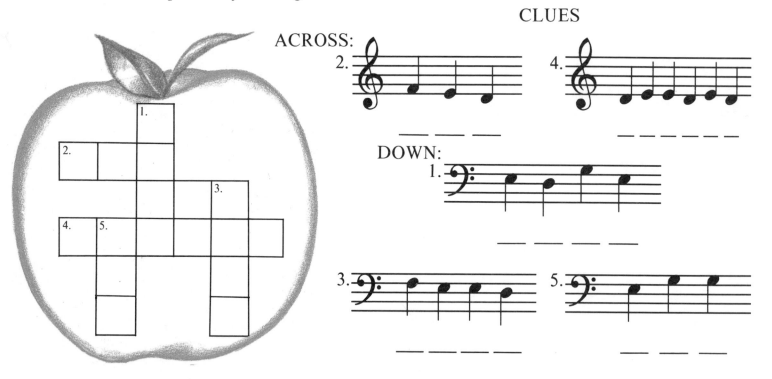

CLUES

ACROSS:

2. ___ ___ ___

4. ___ ___ ___ ___ ___

DOWN:

1. ___ ___ ___ ___

3. ___ ___ ___ ___

5. ___ ___ ___

11. * Look and listen as your teacher plays. Draw the missing notes.

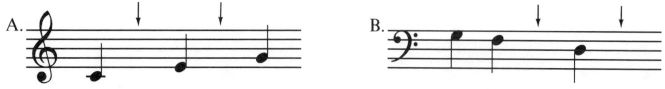

A.

B.

* Music examples for the teacher's use are included in the answers found in the back of this book, pages 45-50.

Use with page 9, LESSONS, Level One.

Melodic and Harmonic Intervals

An INTERVAL is the distance between two tones.

MELODIC INTERVALS are played separately, one at a time. They create MELODIES in music.

HARMONIC INTERVALS are played together. They create HARMONY in music.

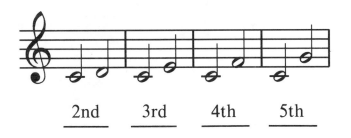

2nd   3rd   4th   5th

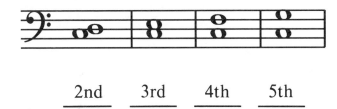

2nd   3rd   4th   5th

12. Name the HARMONIC intervals below. Play and name these intervals.

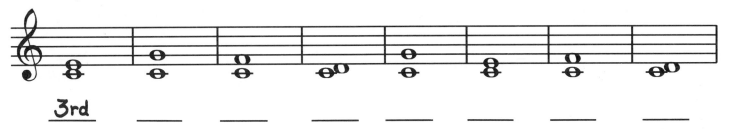

3rd ____ ____ ____ ____ ____ ____ ____

13. Draw a whole note above the given note to make a HARMONIC interval.

3rd   5th   2nd   4th   2nd   3rd

14. Write the name of these MELODIC intervals. Play and sing the note names.

____ ____ ____ ____ ____ ____

*15. Listen as your teacher plays these intervals. In the first blank, write H for harmonic or M for melodic. In the second blank, write the number name of the interval.

A. **H**   **2**   B. ____ ____   C. ____ ____

D. ____ ____   E. ____ ____   F. ____ ____

Use with page 10, LESSONS, Level One.

8

FIRST ENDING

1. Play first time only, then repeat the section.

SECOND ENDING

2. Play the second time, skipping the first ending.

16. A. Follow the bee and play through the 1st ending. Count aloud.

STOP
GO
BACK!

B. Follow the bee and play through the 2nd ending.

THE END.

C. Play this piece, counting aloud.

HARMONIC INTERVAL ACCOMPANIMENT IN C MAJOR

When playing in the C Major position, these two harmonic intervals are often used as accompaniment for the melody:

5th   2nd

17. Play this melody again, using these two harmonic intervals as accompaniment for the melody. Count aloud.

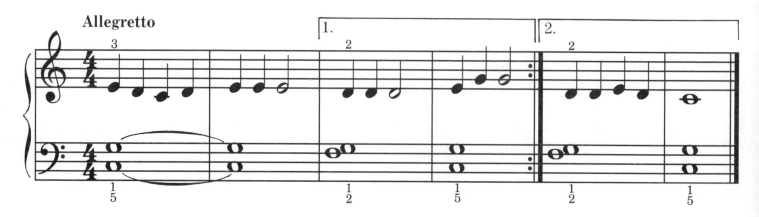

Use with page 11, LESSONS, Level One.

DYNAMICS

mf is the abbreviation for MEZZO FORTE. It means to play **MODERATELY LOUD.**

18. Trace the first *mf* sign below, then draw four more.

mf —— —— —— ——

mp is the abbreviation for MEZZO PIANO. It means to play **MODERATELY SOFT.**

19. Trace the first *mp* sign below, then draw four more.

mp —— —— —— ——

20. Read the words of each piece below. Choose a dynamic sign (*mf* or *mp*) and write it in the box at the beginning of each piece. Trace the harmonic intervals in the bass staff, then play these pieces while counting aloud.

A. **Moderato**

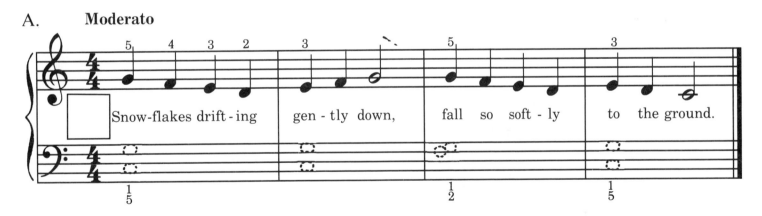

B. **Allegretto**

Use with page 11, LESSONS, Level One.

Tempo Marks

TEMPO MARKS at the beginning of a piece tell us how fast or slow to play the music. Tempo marks are often written in Italian.

ADAGIO slow, at leisure	**ANDANTE** slow, gentle walking tempo	**MODERATO** moderately	**ALLEGRETTO** moderately fast	**ALLEGRO** fast, cheerful

21. Write the tempo mark that matches the rate of speed.

    _____ fast, cheerful

    _____ slow, gentle walking tempo

    _____ moderately fast

    _____ slow, at leisure

    _____ moderately

22. Read the words below and decide if the music should be fast or slow. Choose a tempo mark for each line of music and write it in the blank.

    Play these pieces while counting aloud.

    A. _____

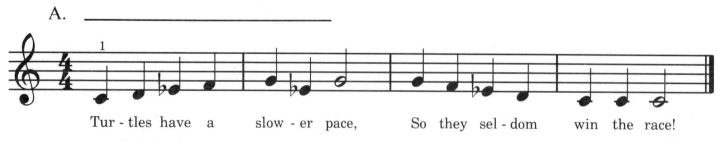

Tur - tles have a slow - er pace, So they sel - dom win the race!

    B. _____

Lit - tle mouse so cute and fur - ry, run so fast, now hur - ry, scur-ry!!

Use with page 12, LESSONS, Level One.

Ritardando (rit.)

Rit. is the abbreviation for the Italian word RITARDANDO. It means to play gradually SLOWER.

23.   Write the abbreviation *rit.* in each blank below.

_____   _____   _____   _____   _____

24.   Play the piece below, gradually slowing down when you see the abbreviation *rit.* Count aloud.

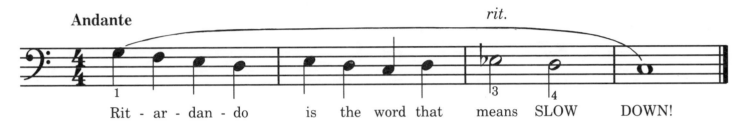

Rit - ar - dan - do   is   the word that   means SLOW   DOWN!

A TEMPO

The words *A TEMPO* often follow a RITARDANDO. *A TEMPO* means to return to the original speed.

25.   Play this piece. Slow down when you see the word *rit.*, and return to the first tempo when you see the words *A Tempo*. Count aloud.

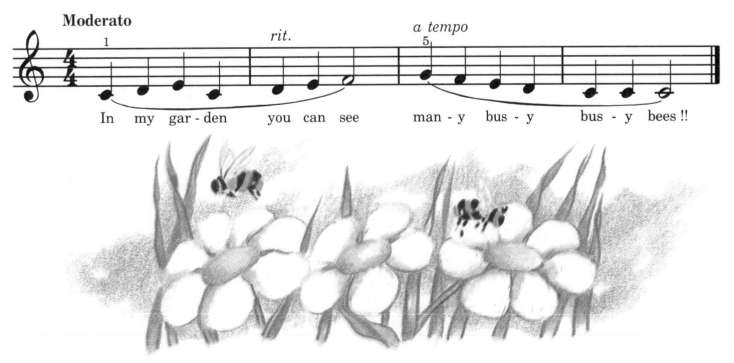

In   my gar - den   you can see   man - y bus - y   bus - y bees !!

Use with page 13, LESSONS, Level One.

Staccato and Legato (Review)

When the note stem goes down, the dot is placed ABOVE the note. ( )

When the note stem goes up, the dot is placed BELOW the note. ( )

26. Draw dots above or below these notes to form staccato notes. Play this piece while counting aloud.

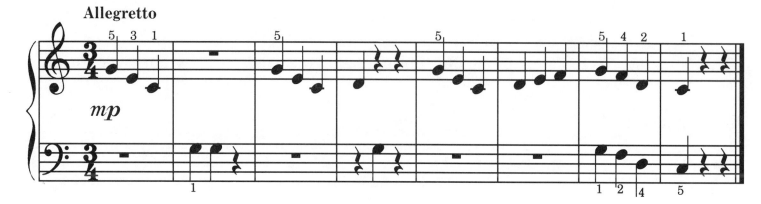

 A SLUR above or below a group of notes means to play LEGATO (smooth and connected).

27. A. Draw slurs BELOW these notes. Connect all the notes found between the rests. Play this piece while counting aloud.

   B. Draw slurs ABOVE these notes. Play this piece while counting aloud.

* 28. Look and listen as your teacher plays. Circle the example you hear. (Circle 1 or 2.)

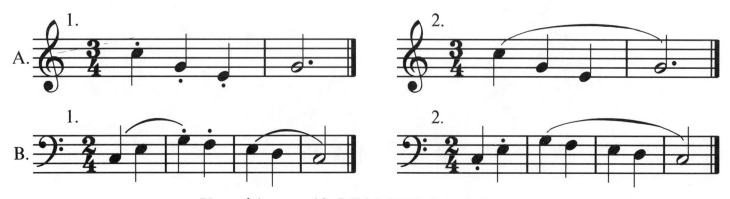

Use with page 13, LESSONS, Level One.

Upbeat

An UPBEAT is the note or notes that come BEFORE the first complete measure of a piece. The missing beats in this incomplete measure are found in the LAST measure of the piece, which is also incomplete.

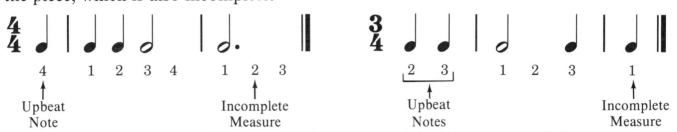

29. Play this piece while counting aloud.

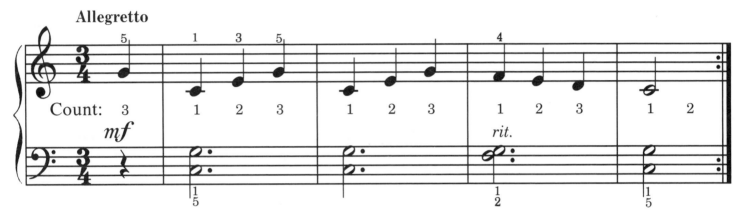

30. Write the beats under the notes below. There is an upbeat in each line. Clap and count aloud.

Use with pages 14-15, LESSONS, Level One.

MIDDLE C POSITION
(Review)

31. Name these notes.

32. In the box on each watering can, write the number of the flower that matches.

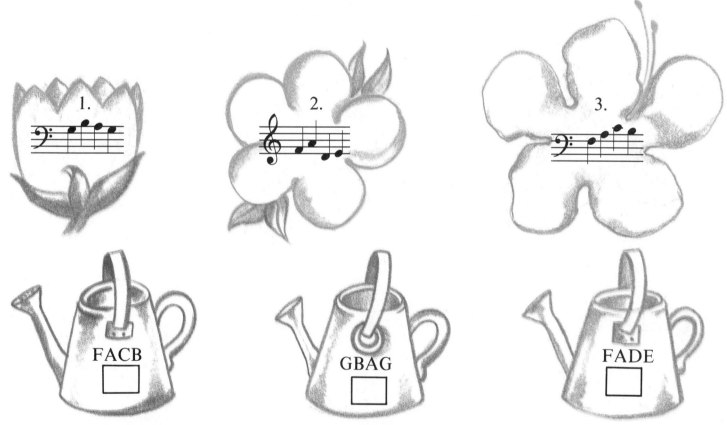

1.

2.

3.

FACB

GBAG

FADE

* 33. Look and listen as your teacher plays. Draw the missing notes.

A.

B.

Use with pages 16-17, LESSONS, Level One.

Tone Balance

Many times one hand will play louder than the other. This is called TONE BALANCE.

34. Tap and count aloud. Tap left hand loudly. Tap right hand softly.

From "Merry-Go-Round," LESSONS, Level One, page 18

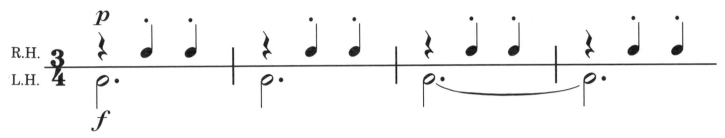

35. Play these measures softly (*p*) with your right hand. Count aloud.

36. Play these measures loudly (*f*) with your left hand. Count aloud.

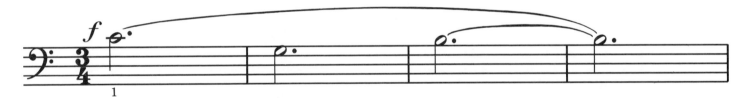

37. Play left hand loudly, right hand softly. Count aloud.

(Finish playing this piece on page 18 in LESSONS, Level One.)

Use with page 18, LESSONS, Level One.

38. First solve the "clues,"then write the answer in the matching blank. For example, for clue number 1, the answer is "Half."

A HAPPY PUPPY

My puppy, "_____ - Pint,"
        1.

ran out of the house, down the

_____ s, and into the _____
2.   3.

yard. What did he _____ to make him
                            4.

run so _____? It was a lovely yellow
         5.

butterfly flitting from flower to flower.

A _____ breeze blew the _____
  6.   7.

across the _____.
        8.

CLUES: Choose from these words:
SEE . . . SOFT . . . FAST . . . BACK . . . GRASS . . . STEP . . . HALF . . . LEAVES

---

1. This (♩) is a _____ note.

2. From one key to the very next key is a half _____.

3. A repeat (:‖) sign means to go _____ to the beginning and play again.

4. Fill in the letter names:

S__ __

5. Allegro means to play _____.

6. *p* means to play _____ ly.

7. Fill in the letter names:

L __ __ V __ S

8. Fill in the letter names:

__ R __ SS

Use with page 18, LESSONS, Level One.

"_____ - Pint" and the
9.

butterfly played _____
10.

until _____ they were getting tired.
11.

"_____ - Pint" gave _____ _____
12.   13.   14.

bark and sat down. It was _____ to _____.
15.   16.

What fun he _____ playing with the butterfly!
17.

CLUES: Choose from these words:
HALF...ONE...TOGETHER...LOUD...HALF...REST...HAD...
GRADUALLY...TIME

---

9.   From one key to the very next key is a _____ step.

10. Notes of HARMONIC intervals are played _____.
(Separately or Together.)

11. Ritardando means to play _____ slower.

12. This (♩.) is a dotted _____ note.

13. This note (♩) receives _____ beat in 4/4 time.

14. 𝑓 means to play _____ ly.

15. This (4/4) is a _____ signature.

16. This (𝄽) is a quarter _____.

17. Fill in the letter names:

H __ __

New G Major Position
HALF STEPS AND WHOLE STEPS

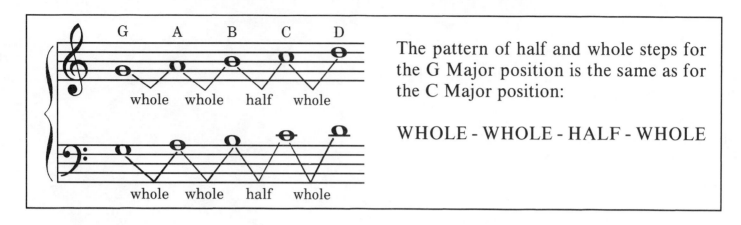

The pattern of half and whole steps for the G Major position is the same as for the C Major position:

WHOLE - WHOLE - HALF - WHOLE

39. Name the notes below. Write H for half step or W for whole step under each pair of notes.

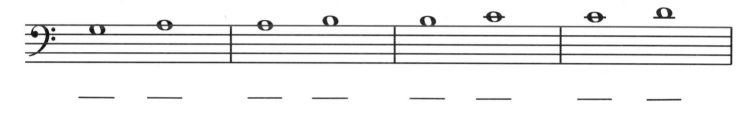

40. On the blanks below the keyboard, write H for half step or W for whole step for the keys that are marked.

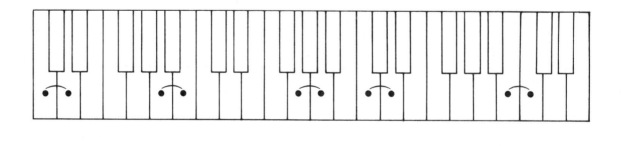

THE G MAJOR KEY SIGNATURE

The key of G Major has one sharp, F♯. It means all Fs are to be played F♯.

KEY SIGNATURE:

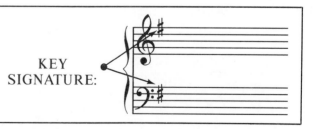

Use with page 19, LESSONS, Level One.

New G Major Position

R.H. 1 2 3 4 5

L.H. 5 4 3 2 1

41. Name these notes.

A.

B.

_____ _____ _____ _____ _____

42. Write the letter names of the notes in the "clues." On the lines under the letters in the grapes, write the number of the clue that matches.

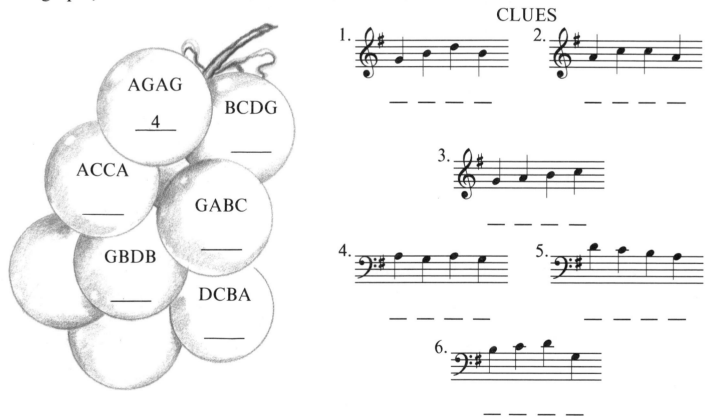

AGAG

_4_

BCDG

_____

ACCA

_____

GABC

_____

GBDB

_____

DCBA

_____

CLUES

1.

_____ _____ _____ _____

2.

_____ _____ _____ _____

3.

_____ _____ _____ _____

4.

_____ _____ _____ _____

5.

_____ _____ _____ _____

6.

_____ _____ _____ _____

* 43. Look and listen as your teacher plays. Draw the missing notes.

A.

B.

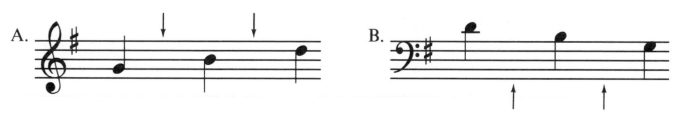

Use with page 20, LESSONS, Level One.

Crescendo and Diminuendo (cresc.) (dim.)

CRESCENDO and DIMINUENDO are DYNAMIC signs. They are placed in music to help the performer play with musical expression.

CRESCENDO (cresc.)
means to play gradually LOUDER.

DIMINUENDO (dim.)
means to play gradually SOFTER.

44. A. Trace this CRESCENDO sign.   B. Trace this DIMINUENDO sign.

45. Trace the crescendo and diminuendo signs below this piece. Play the piece, following the directions for crescendo and diminuendo. Count aloud.

G MAJOR POSITION

46. Name the notes in the G Major position below.

47. Name these notes. They spell words.

Use with pages 21 - 22, LESSONS, Level One.

Fermata

This is the sign for a FERMATA. When placed under or over a note, it means to hold the note longer than its time value.

48.   Trace this FERMATA sign. Draw four more FERMATA signs.

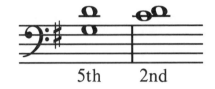

HARMONIC INTERVAL ACCOMPANIMENT IN G MAJOR

When playing in the G Major position, these two harmonic intervals are often used as accompaniment for the melody:

5th   2nd

49.   Copy each harmonic interval in the given blank measures.

5th

2nd

50.   Trace the harmonic intervals in the bass clef. Write the names of the two notes in each harmonic interval on the blanks below. Play this piece while counting aloud.

Andante

* 51.   Listen as your teacher plays two musical examples. Write *cresc.* if the music gets gradually louder, or *dim.* if the music gets gradually softer.

A. _____   B. _____

Use with page 23, LESSONS, Level One.

D.C. al Fine

D.C. al FINE is the abbreviation for the Italian words *DA CAPO AL FINE*. It means to go back to the beginning of the piece and play to the word *FINE*. (*FINE* means "the end" and is pronounced "fee-nay.")

52.　Write the abbreviation ***D.C. al Fine*** three times below.

_____　　_____　　_____

53.　Play this piece. After playing both lines, go back to the beginning and play the first line again, to the word *fine*. Count aloud.

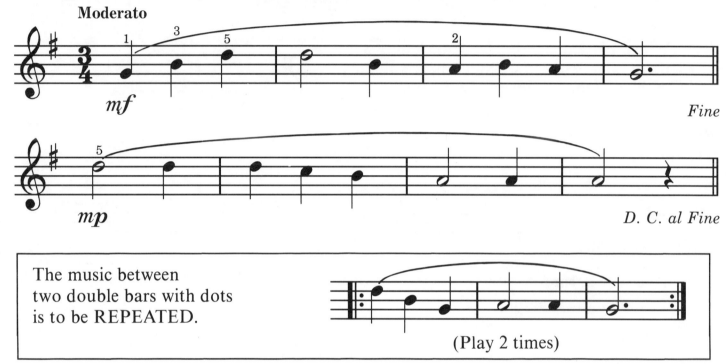

54.　Play this music. Repeat the measures between the double bars with dots. On the repeat, play *piano* (softly). Count aloud.

TEMPO MATCH-UP

55.　Draw a line matching each tempo mark with its correct meaning.

ALLEGRO •　　　　　• moderately

ADAGIO •　　　　　• fast, cheerful

MODERATO •　　　　　• slow, at leisure

Use with page 23, LESSONS, Level One.

Accent >

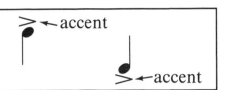

This is an ACCENT mark. When placed over or under a note, it means to play the note LOUDER than the notes before or after it.

56. Draw accent marks over or under these notes.

57. Play this piece. Accent the notes as indicated.

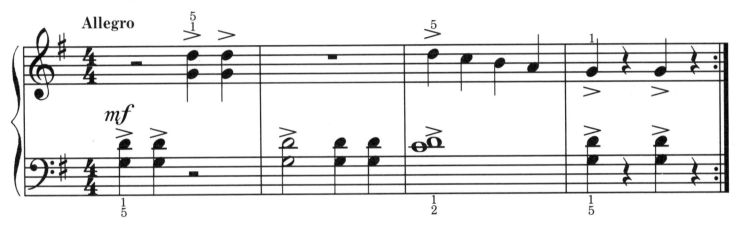

58. Play these harmonic intervals in the G Major position. Name each interval as you play.

59. Name these harmonic intervals.

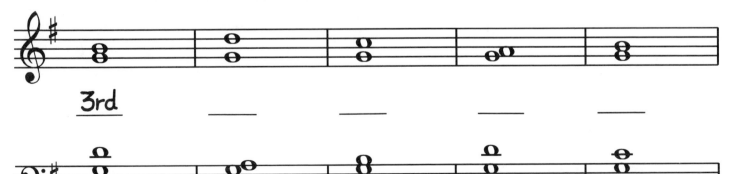

Use with page 24, LESSONS, Level One.

Eighth Notes

This is a single eighth note. It has a flag. It receives one-half of a beat when the quarter note receives one beat.		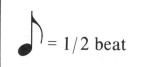

60. Add flags to these quarter notes to make single eighth notes.

Eighth notes are often written in pairs, and are joined together by a beam. Two eighth notes equal one quarter note, and receive one beat in $\frac{2}{4}$, $\frac{3}{4}$ or $\frac{4}{4}$ time.	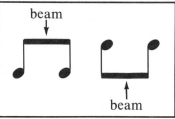	

61. Connect the following pairs of eighth notes with a beam.

Eighth notes may be counted:

    "one-and two-and"
    (1   +   2   +)

or: 1-a 2-a
or: 1-un 2-oo

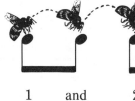

Count: 1   and   2   and   3   and

62. Write the beats under the following rhythms, then clap and count aloud.

1+   2+   1 + 2+   ___ ___   ___ ___

___ ___ ___   ___ ___ ___   ___ ___ ___

Use with page 25, LESSONS, Level One.

Eighth Rest

This is an EIGHTH REST. It has the same time value as one eighth note. $\quad \boldsymbol{\gamma} = 1/2$ beat

63. Trace this eighth rest, then draw four more.

_____   _____   _____   _____   _____

64. Write the beats under these rhythms. Play these rhythms on the keyboard, using any key you choose. Be sure to lift your finger from the key for the rests. Count aloud.

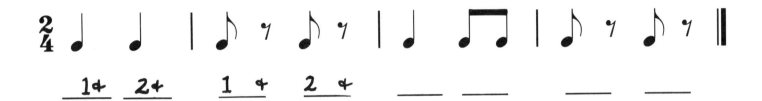

1+   2+   1   +   2   +   ___ ___   ___ ___

___   ___ ___ ___   ___ ___ ___   ___ ___

___   ___ ___ ___   ___ ___ ___   ___ ___

* 65. Listen as your teacher plays a melody. Circle the rhythm pattern you hear.
(Circle A or B).

Use with page 25, LESSONS, Level One.

Low Left Hand G Major Position

(Review)

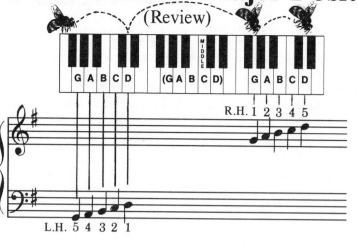

66. Name these notes:

67. Solve the puzzle by naming the notes in the "clues."

CLUES:

ACROSS:

2.

4.

DOWN:

1.

2.    3.

5.    6.

* 68. Look and listen as your teacher plays. Draw the missing notes.

Use with page 26, LESSONS, Level One.

Time Signature Review

2 Top number: 2 beats in each measure	**3** Top number: 3 beats in each measure	**4** Top number: 4 beats in each measure
4 Bottom number: a quarter note receives ONE beat.	**4** Bottom number: a quarter note receives ONE beat.	**4** Bottom number: a quarter note receives ONE beat.

69. Fill in the blanks.

   A. In **4/4** time, there are _____ beats in each measure.

   B. In **2/4** time, a quarter note receives _____ beat.

   C. In **3/4** time, a _____ note receives ONE beat.

   D. In **3/4** time, there are _____ beats in each measure.

   E. In **2/4** time, there are two beats in each _____.

70. Study the rhythms below. Draw the correct time signature at the beginning of each line. Clap and count aloud.

   A.

   B.

   C.

Use with page 26, LESSONS, Level One.

Natural Sign

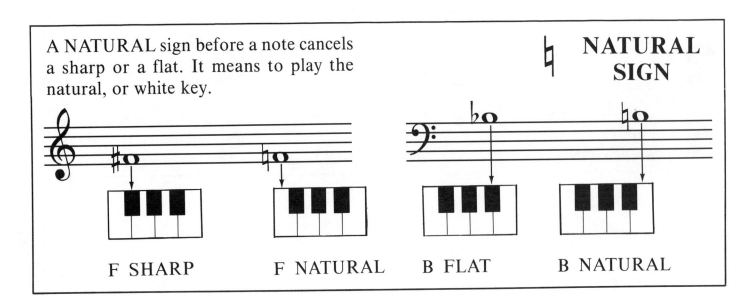

A NATURAL sign before a note cancels a sharp or a flat. It means to play the natural, or white key.

♮ **NATURAL SIGN**

F SHARP   F NATURAL   B FLAT   B NATURAL

71. Trace these natural signs, then draw four more.

72. The "square" in the natural sign is placed on a line (♮) or in a space (♮).
Draw natural signs before these notes.

SHARP, FLAT, and NATURAL REVIEW

73.

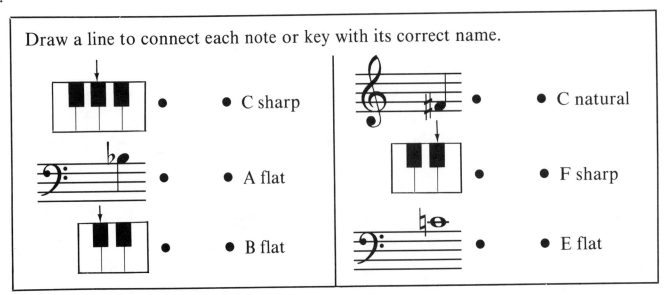

Draw a line to connect each note or key with its correct name.

• C sharp

• A flat

• B flat

• C natural

• F sharp

• E flat

Use with page 27, LESSONS, Level One.

Sharp, Flat, and Natural Signs

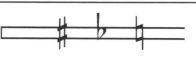

On a line: In a space:

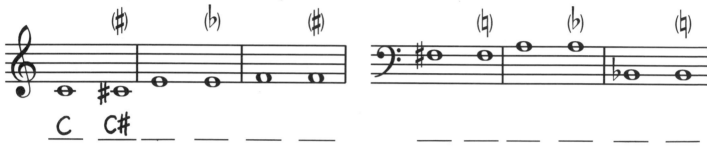

- A sharp RAISES a note one-half step.
  - A flat LOWERS a note one-half step.
    - A natural CANCELS a sharp or a flat.

74. Draw a SHARP, FLAT, OR NATURAL sign before the second note of each measure, as indicated by the sign above each note. Write the name of each note on the blank below. Play these notes and say their letter names aloud.

C   C#   ___   ___   ___   ___   ___   ___

75. Sharps, flats, and naturals are also called ACCIDENTALS. Draw a sharp, flat, or natural sign before each note as indicated. Use the accidental found above or below the note. Play this piece. Count aloud.

ACCIDENTAL BOOGIE

Use with page 27, LESSONS, Level One.

F Major Position
HALF STEPS AND WHOLE STEPS

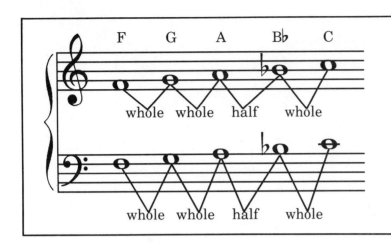

The F Major position has the same pattern of half and whole steps as the C Major and the G Major positions:

WHOLE - WHOLE - HALF - WHOLE

76. Name the keys marked below, then write H for half step or W for whole step under each pair of keys.

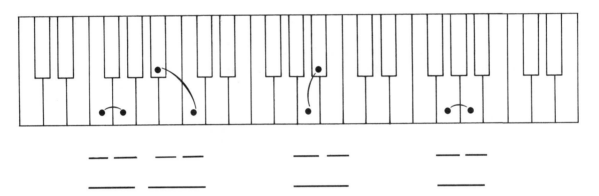

77. Trace the notes in the F Major position. Write H for half step or W for whole step between each pair of notes.

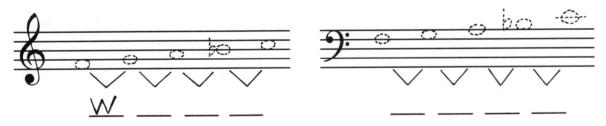

THE F MAJOR KEY SIGNATURE

The key of F Major has one flat, B♭.
It means all Bs are to be played B♭.

KEY SIGNATURE:

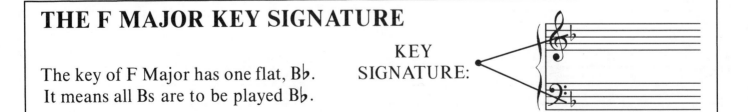

Use with page 28, LESSONS, Level One.

F Major Position

78. Name these notes. Remember to place a flat sign after each B letter name.

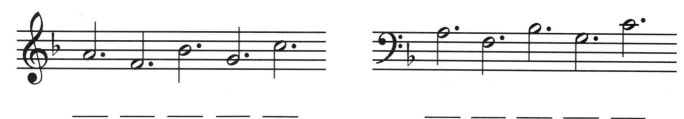

___ ___ ___ ___   ___ ___ ___ ___

79. Write the letter names on the lines under the notes. Read this important message!

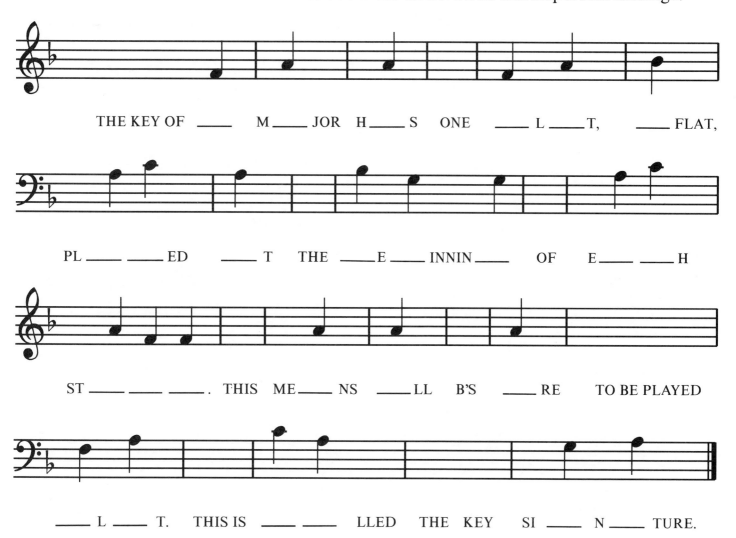

THE KEY OF ___ M ___ JOR H ___ S ONE ___ L ___ T, ___ FLAT,

PL ___ ___ ED ___ T THE ___ E ___ INNIN ___ OF E ___ ___ H

ST ___ ___ ___ . THIS ME ___ NS ___ LL B'S ___ RE TO BE PLAYED

___ L ___ T. THIS IS ___ ___ LLED THE KEY SI ___ N ___ TURE.

Use with pages 29-31, LESSONS, Level One.

8va

The *8va* sign means to play 1 octave, or 8 keys, higher or lower than written.

When *8va* is placed OVER notes, play them 1 octave HIGHER than written.

When *8va* is placed UNDER notes, play them 1 octave LOWER than written.

80.   Play this piece. Follow directions for the *8va* signs. Count aloud.

HARMONIC INTERVAL ACCOMPANIMENT IN F MAJOR

When playing in the F Major position, these two harmonic intervals are often used as accompaniment for the melody:

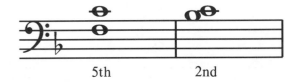

81.   Copy each harmonic interval below in the given blank measures.

82.   Write the name of each harmonic interval in the F Major position. Play these harmonic intervals. Name each interval as you play.

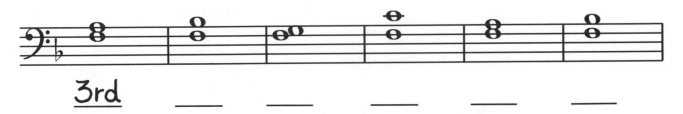

Use with pages 32-33, LESSONS, Level One.

Sharps and Flats

The square part of the sharp sign is placed
on the same line or space as the note.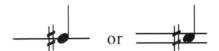

83. Draw a sharp sign before each note, then write the name of each note on the blank
below.

F# ___ ___ ___ ___ ___ ___ ___ ___

The round part of the flat sign is placed
on the same line or space as the note.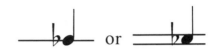

84. Draw a flat sign before each note, then name the notes below.

G♭ ___ ___ ___ ___ ___ ___ ___ ___

When a sharp or a flat sign is placed before a note, that note remains sharp or flat for the
WHOLE measure, unless cancelled by a natural sign.

also F#

also E♭

85. Play the following piece. REMEMBER: The sharp sign lasts for the WHOLE measure.
Count aloud.

2nd time play 8va

Clouds are drift-ing through the sky, Float-ing up they go so high!

Use with pages 32-33, LESSONS, Level One.

86. Solve this puzzle by filling in the blanks of the "clues." Choose your answers from the words in the "puffs of smoke."

STACCATO

FOURTH

MEZZO FORTE

FERMATA

CLUES:

SECOND

DOWN:

1. This (♪) is an eighth _____.
2. The key of F Major has one (♭) _____.
3. A (⌢) _____ means to hold the note longer than written.
4. This ≣ is a harmonic interval of a _____.
6. *8va* means to play 8 notes or an _____ higher or lower.

OCTAVE

ACROSS:

3. This ≣ is a harmonic interval of a _____.

THIRD

FLAT

5. This ≣ is a harmonic interval of a _____.

7. *mf* is the symbol for _____ _____ which means

FIFTH

to play medium loud.

8. A dot (♩ ♩) over or under the note means to play _____.
9. This ≣ is a harmonic interval of a _____.

NOTE

How To Transpose

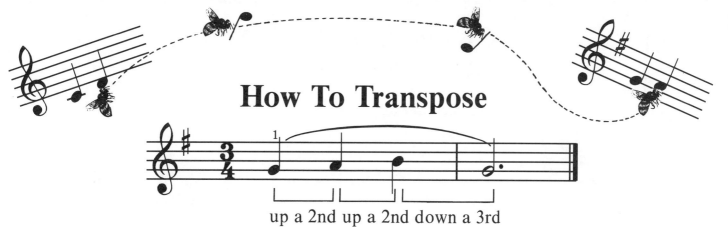

up a 2nd up a 2nd down a 3rd

87. Study this music, then answer the questions below.

   1. What is the beginning note? _____ Is it the same as the key in which the music is written? _____

   2. How does the first note move to the second note:
      what melodic interval? _____ , up or down? _____

   3. How does the second note move to the third note:
      what melodic interval? _____ , up or down? _____

   4. How does the third note move to the fourth note:
      what melodic interval? _____ , up or down? _____

   5. What is the value of each note?   ♩ ♩ ♩ | ♩.

   6. Play this music.   ___   ___   ___   ___

88. Transpose the same music to the KEY OF C MAJOR. Play the music.

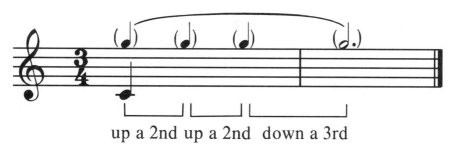

up a 2nd up a 2nd down a 3rd

89. Transpose the same music to the KEY OF F MAJOR. Play the music.

Use with pages 35-36, LESSONS, Level One.

Changing Positions

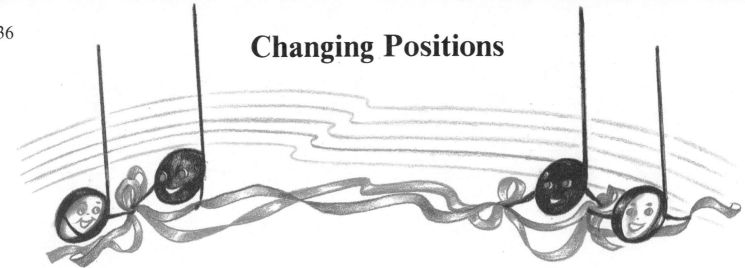

90. On the line below each note, write the letter name. Above the staff write the name of the correct hand position. Then play while counting aloud.

Excerpt from "Changing Partners," LESSONS, pages 38, 39

_____C_____ Position   _____ Position

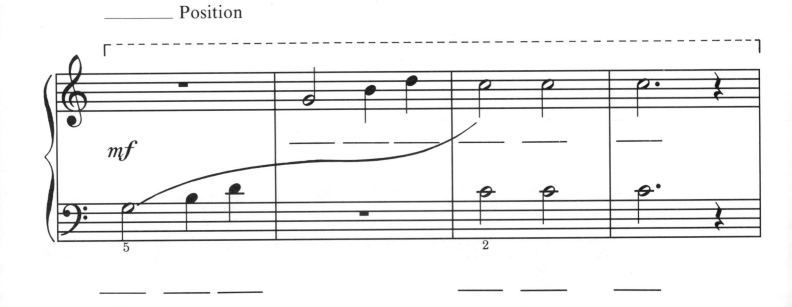

_____ Position

Use with pages 37-39, LESSONS, Level One.

Position Review

91. Study the notes on each staff, then fill in the blank to name the position. On each keyboard, write the letter names of that same position. Mark the left hand and right hand notes with a bracket as illustrated in the example, and write the finger numbers of each hand.

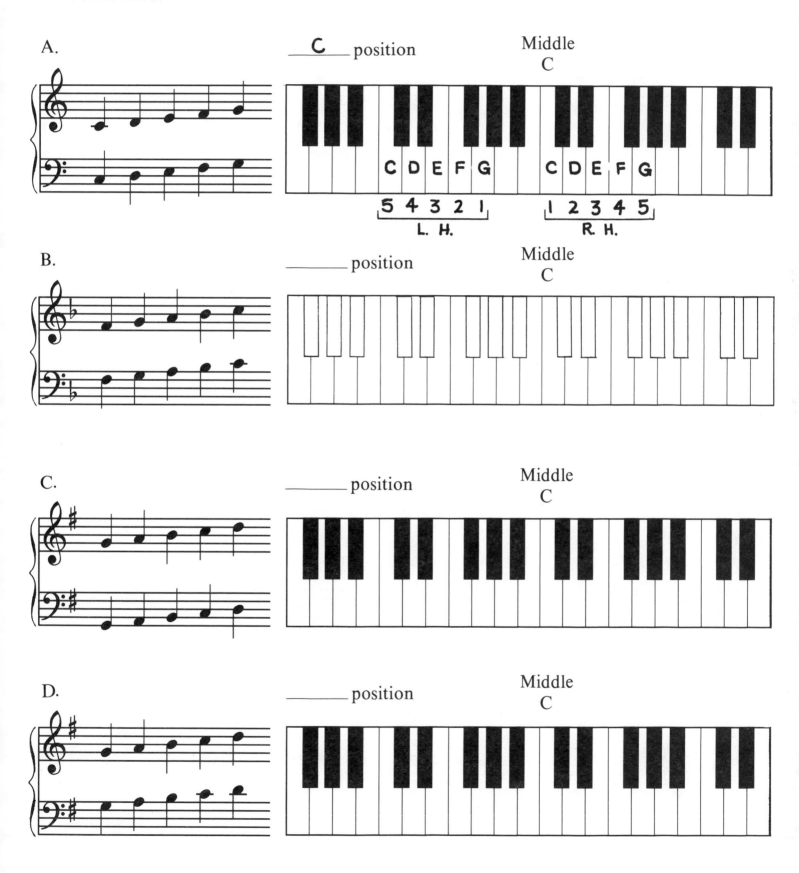

Use with page 40, LESSONS, Level One.

Review: Keys of C, F, and G Major

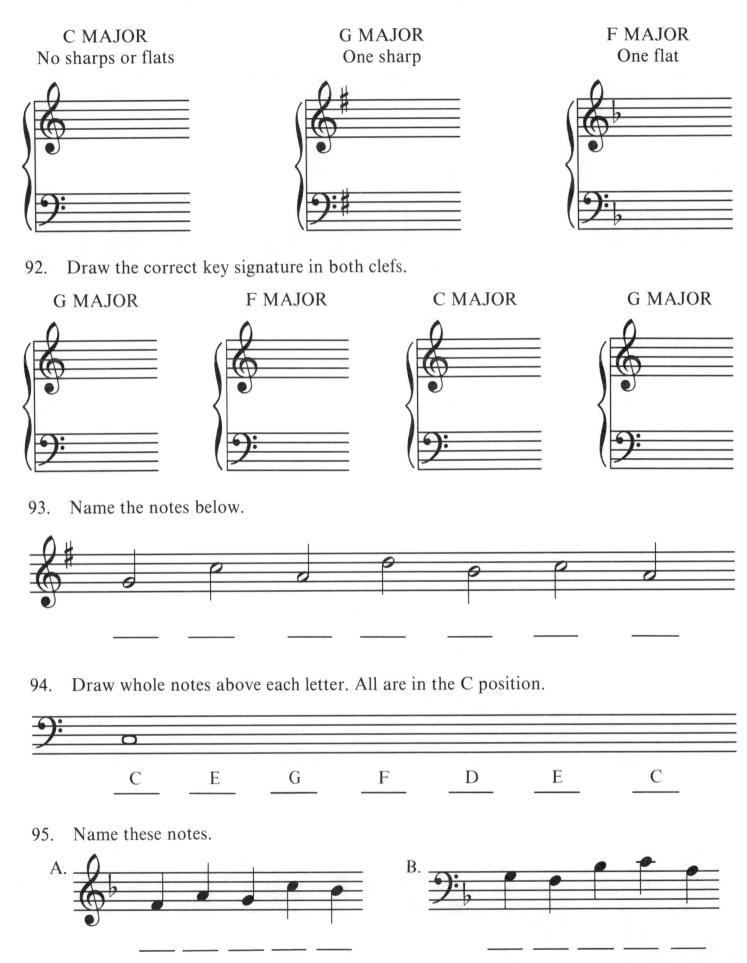

C MAJOR
No sharps or flats

G MAJOR
One sharp

F MAJOR
One flat

92. Draw the correct key signature in both clefs.

G MAJOR   **F MAJOR**   **C MAJOR**   **G MAJOR**

93. Name the notes below.

94. Draw whole notes above each letter. All are in the C position.

C   E   G   F   D   E   C

95. Name these notes.

A.

B.

Use with page 40, LESSONS, Level One.

The Damper Pedal

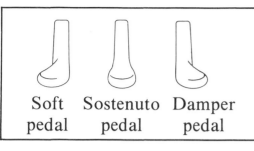

Soft pedal Sostenuto pedal Damper pedal

The DAMPER PEDAL is the pedal on the right.

The DAMPER PEDAL sustains tones.

This is the pedal sign. It shows when to press and lift the pedal.

PRESS   HOLD   LIFT

96. Draw two pedal signs.

97. Play this piece. Use your right foot to press and release the damper pedal. Keep your heel on the floor when pedaling. Count aloud.

CLIMBING
(Changing positions)

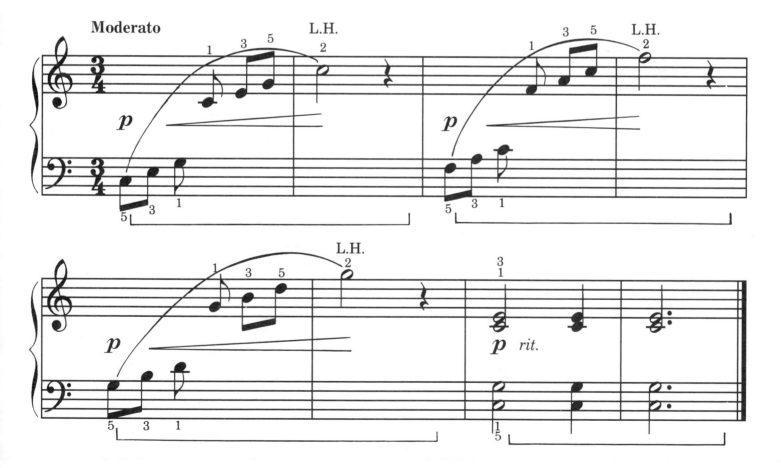

Use with pages 41-43, LESSONS, Level One.

Form in Music

MUSIC FORM is the pattern of a piece. The patterns in music may be alike, similar, or different.

98. Play this piece. Decide which measures are alike, similar, or different. Write your answers in the blanks below.

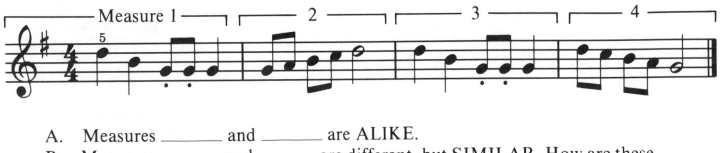

A. Measures _____ and _____ are ALIKE.

B. Measures _____ and_____ are different, but SIMILAR. How are these

2 measures similar?_____

99. Play this piece. Answer the questions below.

A. Lines_____ and_____ are exactly alike.

B. Line_____ is similar to lines 2 and 4.

C. Line_____ is completely different from the other three lines.

Use with pages 44-45, LESSONS, Level One.

Music Symbols and Terms — Review

100. Write the number of each snowflake beside its definition.

1. ♯

2. *8va*

3. ♫

4. coda

5. ♭

6. legato

7. ♼

8 *dim.*

9. ♪

10. *cresc.*

11. *a tempo*

12. *D.C. al fine*

_____ Eighth rest

_____ Resume original speed

_____ A sharp sign _____ A flat sign

_____ An added ending

_____ Smooth and connected

_____ Play gradually louder _____ Play gradually softer

_____ Return to beginning and play to *fine*

_____ Play one octave higher or lower _____ Two eighth notes

_____ Note to be played with stress (louder)

Use with pages 46-49, LESSONS, Level One.

Transposition

Excerpt from "F Position Fishin'," LESSONS, Level One, page 30.

101. Trace the letter names of the keys in this position. Play these measures.

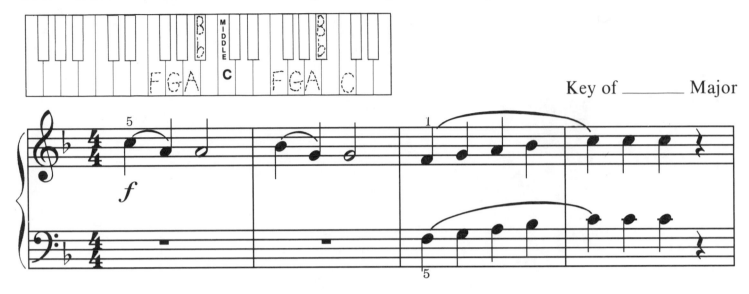

Key of _____ Major

102. Write the letter names of the keys in this position. Play these measures.

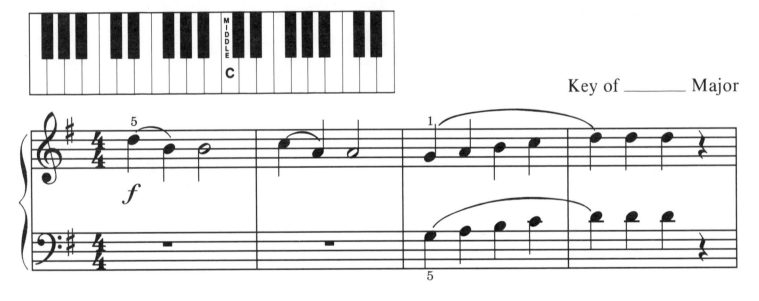

Key of _____ Major

103. Write the letter names of the keys in this position. Play these measures.

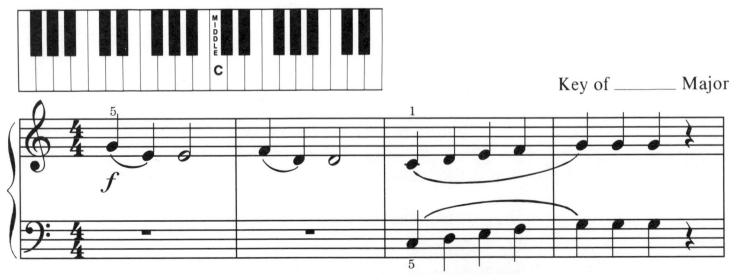

Key of _____ Major

Use with pages 50-53, LESSONS, Level One.

Note and Interval Review

104. Complete this story. Write the letter name of each single note, and the number name of each harmonic interval.

A.

The new commander of the space ship was named ___ ___ ___ ___.

B.

He was the captain of all the space robots.

His robot co-captain was named ___ ___ ___ ___.

Together they skillfully guided the space craft through the universe.

Their little space dog, named

C.

___ ___ ___ ___ ,

barked happily as the planets and stars seemed to float past the windows of the space craft.

Soon their mission was ended, and they all returned safely back to

D.

___ ___ ___ ___ , which was their space station on earth.

E.

F.

G.

___ ___ ___ , ___ ___ ___ ___ , and ___ ___ ___ ___

were all very happy to be back on earth once more !!

Use after page 53, LESSONS, Level One.

*Listening Skills

Listen as your teacher plays, and write your answers below.

105. Write M for melodic intervals or H for harmonic intervals.

    A. _____ B. _____ C. _____ D. _____

    E. _____

106. Name the interval you hear. Write 2nd, 3rd, 4th, or 5th.

    A. _____ B. _____ C. _____ D. _____

107. Choose a tempo mark for this music. Write Adagio or Allegro.

    A. _____ B. _____

108. Write *cresc.* if this music gets gradually louder, or *dim.* if it gets gradually softer.

109. Which rhythm pattern do you hear? (Circle A or B.)

A.

B.

Use after page 53, LESSONS, Level One.

ANSWERS AND TEACHER'S LISTENING EXAMPLES,
Level One

PAGE 3

1.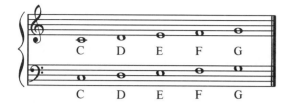

2. Explain this time signature:
   3 ← means there are 3 beats in each measure.
   4 ← means the quarter note receives one beat.

3. Write the number of beats each note or rest receives in 4/4 time.

4.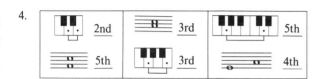

PAGE 4

5. A. C, G, F♯, A, B♭, D, C, E
   B. C, A, B♭, E, F♯, D, C, G

6. A. BEEF, B. CABBAGE, C. ACE, D. BEAD,
   E. BAGGAGE, F. FED

PAGE 5

7. A.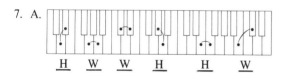
   H   W   W   H   H   W

   B.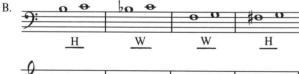
   H   W   W   H

8.

PAGE 6

9. A. D, G, E, C, F   B. D, G, E, C, F

10. ACROSS: 2. FED, 4. DEEDED
    DOWN: 1. EDGE, 3. FEED, 5. EGG

* 11. TEACHER'S LISTENING EXAMPLES:
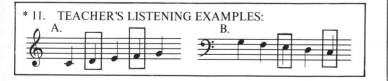

PAGE 7

12.
    3rd 5th 4th 2nd 5th 3rd 4th 2nd

13.
    3rd 5th 2nd 4th 2nd 3rd

14.
    4th 3rd 5th 2nd 5th 4th

* 15.   TEACHER'S LISTENING EXAMPLES
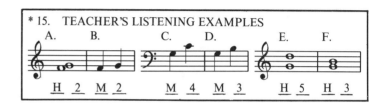
    H 2   M 2   M 4   M 3   H 5   H 3

PAGE 8

16. Students play as directed.

17. Students play as directed.

PAGE 9

18. *mf*   *mf*   *mf*   *mf*   *mf*

19. *mp*   *mp*   *mp*   *mp*   *mp*

20. A.  *mp*   B. *mf*

PAGE 10

21. *Allegro* _____ fast, cheerful
    Andante _____ slow, gentle walking tempo
    Allegretto _____ moderately fast
    Adagio _____ slow, at leisure
    Moderato _____ moderately

22. Students choose tempo marks. More than one answer may be correct.

46

PAGE 11

23. _rit._   _rit._   _rit._   _rit._   _rit._

24. Students play as directed.
25. Students play as directed.

PAGE 12

26.

27. A.

B.

* 28.   TEACHER'S LISTENING EXAMPLES

PAGE 13

29. Students play as directed.

30.

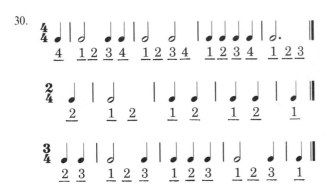

PAGE 14

31.

G D E C F   G B C A F

32.

* 33.   TEACHER'S LISTENING EXAMPLES

A.      B. 

PAGE 15

34. Students tap and count as directed.
35. Students play softly as directed.
36. Students play loudly as directed.
37. Students play hands together as directed.

PAGES 16, 17

38. 1. Half, 2. step, 3. back, 4. see, 5. fast, 6. soft, 7. leaves, 8. grass, 9. Half, 10. together, 11. gradually, 12. Half, 13. one, 14. loud, 15. time, 16. rest, 17. had.

PAGE 18

39.

G A   A B   B C   C D
W   W   H   W

40.

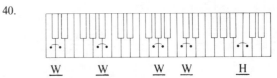

W   W   W   W   H

PAGE 19

41.
B G C D A   G C A D B

42. 1. GBDB, 2. ACCA, 3. GABC, 4. AGAG, 5. DCBA,
6. BCDG

* 43. TEACHER'S LISTENING EXAMPLES
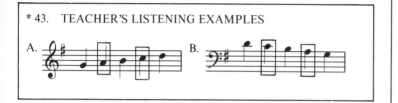

PAGE 20

44. A.    B.

45. Students trace and play as directed.

46.
G B A D C A   G B D A C G

47. A. CAB, BAD   B. BAG, DAB

PAGE 21

48.

49.
5th   2nd

Andante

50.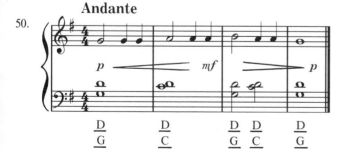
D / G   D / C   D / G   D / C   D / G

* 51. TEACHER'S LISTENING EXAMPLES
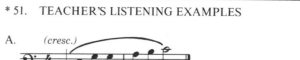

PAGE 22

52. D.C. al Fine   D.C. al Fine   D.C. al Fine

53. Students play as directed.

54. Students play as directed.

55. ALLEGRO - fast, cheerful
MODERATO - moderately
ADAGIO - slow, at leisure

PAGE 23

56.

57. Students play as directed.

58. Students play and name intervals as directed.

59.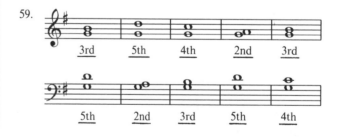
3rd   5th   4th   2nd   3rd
5th   2nd   3rd   5th   4th

PAGE 24

60.

61.

62.

48

63.

64.

*65. TEACHER'S LISTENING EXAMPLES

B.

66.

D A C G B   D A C G B

67. ACROSS: 2. DAB 4. ADA
DOWN: 1. BAD, 2. DAD, 3. BAG, 5. ADD, 6. ADA

*68. TEACHER'S LISTENING EXAMPLES

A.

B.

69. A. four, B. one, C. quarter, D. three, E. measure,

70. A. **3/4**   B. **4/4**   C. **2/4**

71.

72.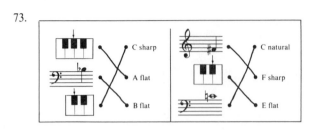

73.

74.

C C♯   E E♭   F F♯   F♯ F♮   A A♭   B♭ B♮

75. **Accidental Boogie**
Allegretto

76.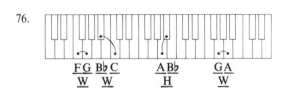

F G B♭ C   A B♭   G A
 W   W   H   W

77.

W W H W   W W H W

PAGE 31

78.

    A F Bb G C   A F Bb G C

79. THE KEY OF F MAJOR HAS ONE FLAT, B FLAT, PLACED AT THE BEGINNING OF EACH STAFF. THIS MEANS ALL B'S ARE TO BE PLAYED FLAT. THIS IS CALLED THE KEY SIGNATURE.

PAGE 32

80. Students play piece as directed.

81.

      5th   2nd

82.

   3rd   4th   2nd   5th   3rd   4th

PAGE 33

83.

  F# D# G# C# A# D# C# E# B# F#

84.

  Gb Cb Db Ab Ab Eb Bb Fb Db Bb

85. Students play piece as directed.

PAGE 34

86. DOWN: 1. NOTE, 2. FLAT, 3. FERMATA, 4. THIRD,
             6. OCTAVE
    ACROSS: 3. FIFTH, 5. FOURTH, 7. MEZZO FORTE,
             8. STACCATO, 9. SECOND

PAGE 35

87. 1. G, yes,   2. 2nd, up,   3. 2nd, up,   4. 3rd, down,
    5. 1 beat, 1 beat, 1 beat, 3 beats.   6. Play.

88.

     up a 2nd up a 2nd down a 3rd

89.

PAGE 36

90.

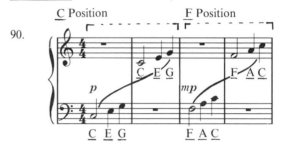

PAGE 37

91. B. F position

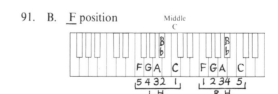

C. Low G position

D. G position

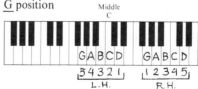

PAGE 38

92.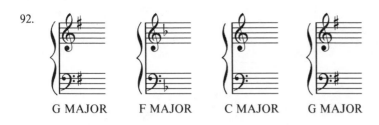

G MAJOR   F MAJOR   C MAJOR   G MAJOR

93.

G   C   A   D   B   C   A

94.

C   E   G   F   D   E   C

95.   A. F, A, G, C, B♭   B. G, F, B♭, C, A

PAGE 39

96.

97.   Students play as directed.

PAGE 40

98.   A. 1 and 3,   B. 2 and 4, Both measures use same
        notes. Measure 2 steps UP, Measure 4 steps DOWN.

99.   A. 2 and 4,   B. 1,   C. 3

PAGE 41

100.   _7_   Eighth rest
       _11_   Resume original speed
       _1_   A sharp sign
       _5_   A flat sign
       _4_   An added ending
       _6_   Smooth & connected
       _10_   Play gradually louder
       _8_   Play gradually softer
       _12_   Return to beginning and play to fine
       _2_   Play one octave higher or lower
       _3_   Two eighth notes
       _9_   Note to be played with stress (louder).

PAGE 42

101. 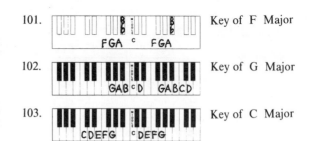   Key of F Major

102.   Key of G Major

103.   Key of C Major

PAGE 43

104.   A. A 2 D 3
       B. C 4 B 5
       C. B 5 C 3
       D. D C G 2
       E. A 2 D 3
       F. C 4 B 5
       G. B 5 C 3

PAGE 44

* TEACHER'S LISTENING EXAMPLES

105. A.   B.   C.   D.   E.

Harmonic Melodic   Melodic Harmonic   Harmonic

106. A.   B.   C.   D.

2nd   3rd   5th   4th

107. A.   Allegro

      B.   Adagio

108.

dim.

109.   B.